First Facts™

Health Matters

Juvenile Diabetes

by Jason Glaser

Consultant:
James R. Hubbard, MD
Fellow in the American Academy of Pediatrics
Iowa Medical Society
West Des Moines, Iowa

Capstone
press®

Mankato, Minnesota

First Facts is published by Capstone Press
151 Good Counsel Drive, P.O. Box 669, Mankato, Minnesota 56002.
www.capstonepress.com

Library of Congress Cataloging-in-Publication Data
Glaser, Jason.
     Juvenile diabetes / by Jason Glaser.
      p. cm.—(First facts. Health matters)
     Summary: "Describes juvenile diabetes, why it occurs, and how it is diagnosed and
treated"—Provided by publisher.
     Includes bibliographical references and index.
     ISBN-13: 978-0-7368-6392-6 (hardcover)
     ISBN-10: 0-7368-6392-3 (hardcover)
     1. Diabetes in children—Juvenile literature. I. Title. II. Series.
RJ420.D5G53 2007
618.92'462—dc22   2006002820

Editorial Credits
Shari Joffe, editor; Biner Design, designer; Juliette Peters, set designer; Jo Miller, photo researcher;
     Scott Thoms, photo editor

Photo Credits
BananaStock, Ltd., 11, 18–19
Capstone Press/Karon Dubke, cover (foreground), 1, 8–9, 21
CNRI/Photo Researchers, Inc., cover (background)
Corbis/Bill Schild, 10; Karen Kasmauski, 13
Photo Researchers, Inc./Coneyl Jay, 14; Richard T. Nowitz, 20; Science Photo Library, 16
Shutterstock/GeoM, 4; Radu Razvan, 15
Superstock/Hank Grebe, 7

1 2 3 4 5 6 11 10 09 08 07 06

Table of Contents

Signs of Juvenile Diabetes

You're thirsty all the time. You often need to use the bathroom, even at night. You're very hungry and eat well, but you're losing weight. All day long you feel tired. These are signs of **juvenile** diabetes.

What Is Juvenile Diabetes?

Our bodies get the energy we need from sugars in food. This sugar gets from our blood to our cells because of **insulin**. Insulin is made in an organ called the **pancreas**.

People with juvenile diabetes have trouble making insulin. Their bodies can't use the sugar needed for energy.

Fact!

In people with diabetes, the body starts using fat cells and muscle for energy. That's why kids with untreated diabetes lose weight.

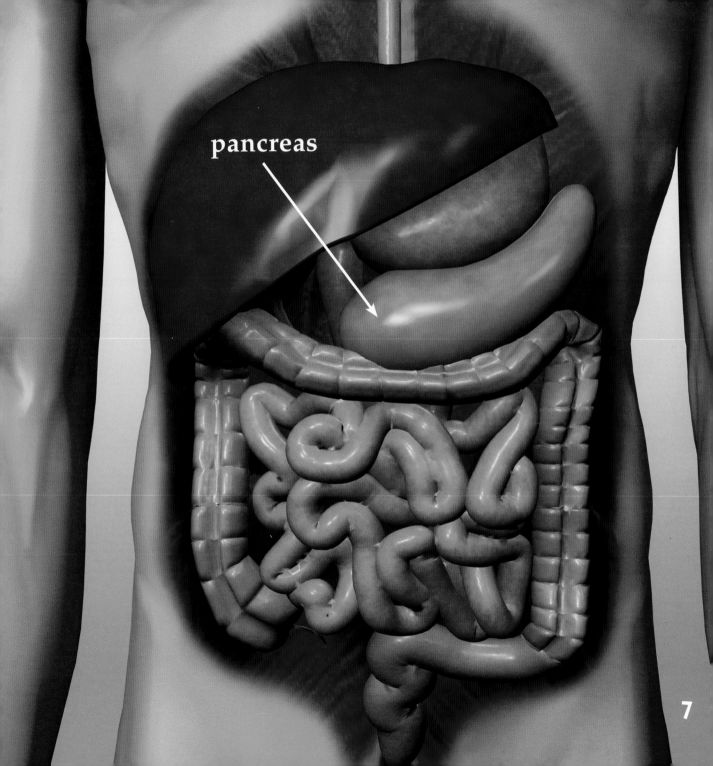

pancreas

How Do Kids Get It?

No one knows for sure how kids get juvenile diabetes. Sometimes it runs in families. Some people's bodies attack the cells that make insulin. Doctors have noticed that this sometimes starts after a person has had certain **viruses**.

Fact!

Some people believe you can get diabetes from eating too much sugar. Too much sugar can be bad for you, but it will not give you diabetes.

What Else Could It Be?

Other things can cause the **symptoms** of diabetes. Hot weather, exercise, or eating salty foods can make you thirsty.

Being tired all the time may not mean you have diabetes. It could just mean you don't get enough sleep at night.

Should Kids See a Doctor?

Kids who think they may have diabetes should see a doctor. Doctors can do tests to see how much sugar is in your blood. If your sugar levels are too high, it means your body can't use the sugar in the food you eat. You have diabetes.

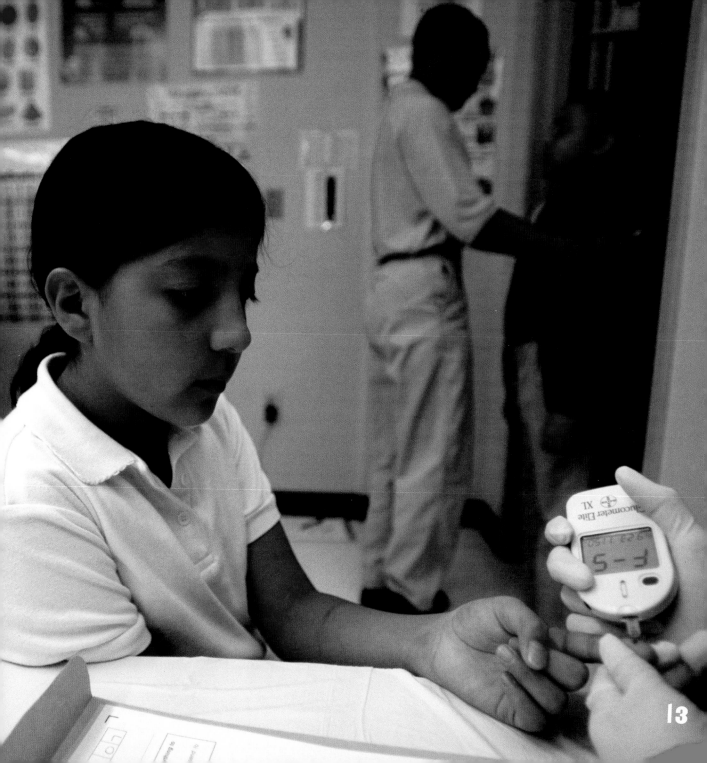

Treatment

Kids who have juvenile diabetes need to take insulin regularly all their lives. It is usually taken before eating or going to bed.

Kids must also test their blood sugar a few times a day. If it is too high, more insulin is needed. If it's too low, they may need to eat a sugary food.

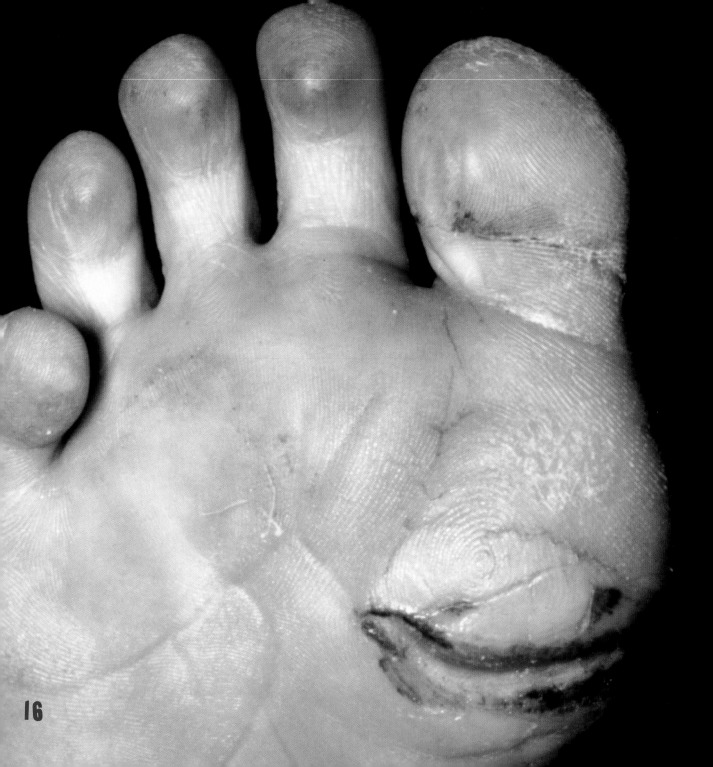

16

What Happens Without Treatment?

Large amounts of sugar in the bloodstream can damage nerves. Hands and feet may lose feeling and get **infected**. People can also have eye problems or go blind. Without insulin, a person with diabetes can go into a **coma** or even die.

Fact!
Scientists learned how to make insulin in 1922. Now people with diabetes can live a long time.

Staying Healthy

There is no cure for juvenile diabetes. But kids with diabetes can live healthy lives if they take good care of themselves. Paying close attention to blood sugar levels is important. Eating a balanced diet and limiting sweets can also help control diabetes.

Amazing but True!

The pancreas has cells that create insulin. Doctors have experimented with putting cells from a healthy person into a person with juvenile diabetes. In some cases, people who received these donated cells started producing insulin again.

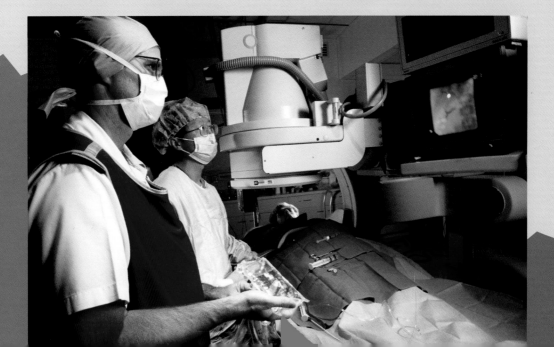

Hands On:
Old Diabetes Test

What You Need

water   small spoon
lemon juice   3 bottle caps
1 teaspoon (5 mL) of sugar   an anthill outside

What You Do

1. Fill one bottle cap with water.
2. Fill the second bottle cap half with water and half with lemon juice.
3. Fill the third bottle cap almost full of water. Then add 1 teaspoon (5 mL) of sugar to the water. Stir the sugar and water together with the spoon.
4. Set the three bottle caps so that they make a triangle around the anthill. Each bottle cap should be about 1 foot (30.5 centimeters) away from the anthill.
5. Watch how the ants move around the bottle caps.

Which liquid did the ants move toward? Thousands of years ago, Greek doctors tested for diabetes by pouring the patient's urine near an anthill. Urine becomes sweeter when there is more sugar in it. If the ants were attracted to the urine, the person had diabetes.

Glossary

coma (KOH-muh)—a state of deep unconsciousness from which it is very hard to wake up

infected (in-FEK-tid)—filled with germs or viruses

insulin (IN-suh-luhn)—a substance made in the pancreas that helps the body use sugar

juvenile (JOO-vuh-nuhl)—describing young people

pancreas (PAN-kree-uhss)—an organ near the stomach that makes insulin

symptom (SIMP-tuhm)—something that shows you have an illness

virus (VY-russ)—a germ that copies itself inside the body's cells

Read More

Gray, Shirley Wimbish. *Living with Diabetes.* Living Well. Chanhassen, Minn.: Child's World, 2003

Stewart, Gail B. *Diabetes.* Kidhaven Science Library. San Diego: Kidhaven Press, 2003.

Internet Sites

FactHound offers a safe, fun way to find Internet sites related to this book. All of the sites on FactHound have been researched by our staff.

Here's how:

1. Visit *www.facthound.com*

2. Choose your grade level.

3. Type in this book ID **0736863923** for age-appropriate sites. You may also browse subjects by clicking on letters, or by clicking on pictures and words.

4. Click on the **Fetch It** button.

FactHound will fetch the best sites for you!

Index